TASTEFULLY BLENDED

❧

CRUNCHY TUBIE MAMA

Copyright © 2018 Crunchy Tubie Mama
All rights reserved. No part of this book may be reproduced in any form or by any electronic or mechanical means, including information storage and retrieval systems, without written permission from the author, except in the case of a reviewer, who may quote brief passages embodied in critical articles or in a review.

❀ Created with Vellum

*This book is dedicated to
Weronika Brill and Jennifer Batts
for teaching me how to make
blending fun*

D and Battboy are forever in my heart.

ALSO BY CRUNCHY TUBIE MAMA

Visit crunchytubiemamabooks.com
to find more books by Crunchy Tubie Mama.

Crunchy Tubie Mama has written many books for children and adults aimed at making healthy living doable and fun.

Illustrated children's books, fantasy books for older children and teens, and fiction and non-fiction books for adults can all be found at Crunchy Tubie Mama Books.

MY JOURNEY

I SAT and rubbed my belly as I dreamed of the baby growing inside. I had just chosen a name: Bradley. There was so much I imagined for his future. I dreamed of of his birth, our celebratory few days in the hospital, and our triumphant return home. I dreamed of cuddling up and feeding him from a bottle.

As much as I wanted to breastfeed, medication I need to survive would prevent me from doing so. I was disappointed, but looked forward to weaning my son onto a healthy, natural diet based mostly on whole plant foods after a year of bottle feeding. I believed I had it all figured out as many idealistic pregnant mothers tend to do.

Reality turned out to be quite different. A series of medical conditions I had never even heard of were soon to enter our lives. The first of these conditions is called HELLP syndrome, causing Bradley to be born nearly 3 months early. He weighed 1 pound, 14 ounces at birth. Next came the diagnosis of tetralogy of fallot, a congenital heart defect. Next, came NEC. Then, a stroke.

Of course, I had heard of a stroke before, but I had not realized babies could have them. The combination of all of these diagnoses lead to multiple bowel and heart surgeries. All of these events, together, lead to the final diagnosis I had not heard of prior to my son's birth: oral aversion.

So much of what I had envisioned for my son did not come true. He spent 165 very long days in the hospital before coming home for the first time. He went back into the hospital multiple times. He never drank from a bottle. Like many babies who have endured extreme medical crises, Bradley developed a sensory disorder called oral aversion. Any touch in or around his mouth resulted in gagging and vomiting. He was unable to eat at all.

Many people have a hard time imagining a child that simply cannot eat. Regularly barraged with unsolicited and unrealistic advice on how to get my orally-aversed child to eat, I sat in devastation. Most people simply did not understand that oral aversion is not treated by feeding "yummy" foods or by suddenly cutting off tube feedings.

"Oh, he won't starve to death!" I was told again and again. Indeed, he absolutely would have starved to death. Bradley's oral aversion was so extreme that he could not tolerate any stimulation to his mouth. He truly was incapable of eating or drinking anything at all. And he stayed that way for a long, long time.

Feeding therapy yielded minimal progress and, often, none at all. Two years passed. Finally, after a long and much needed break from feeding therapy, Bradley's speech therapist and I decided together that it was time to begin again. Shortly afterward, she resigned to accept a new position elsewhere. I felt completely lost.

I began my search for a new therapist and was thrilled to find a local clinic very experienced with children with oral aversion as severe as my son's was. I entered the clinic feeling hopelessness and despair. I could not even imagine my son eating. I could no longer picture it in my mind. But, after meeting his new therapist and completing his evaluation, my sense of hope was renewed.

She saw many positive aspects about Bradley's relationship with food. For example, while he once could not even see a spoon without gagging or vomiting, he now could play with spoons. Food could be placed in front of him, and he would be ok. Indeed, many children with oral aversion cannot be anywhere near food or they will gag or vomit. She believed he was ready and would do well.

I cried the entire way home as I embraced a sense of hope once again. Could she be right? Was Bradley finally going to eat? Could this really be true? I had to believe it was. And so, we began driving to downtown Chicago twice per week with the faith and belief that Bradley would become able to eat. During that time, I was informed by a dietitian that another dream for my son would not come true.

I was told Bradley would not be able to eat a balanced diet. He would have to eat foods I did not want to feed him. I would have to be ok with him consuming large amounts of sugar. I would have to let go of my desire to feed my son the diet I'd imagined during pregnancy. That is just the way it was. Or was it?

I began to do some research and could not find any data in the scientific literature to support this idea that children with oral aversion simply had to eat foods that were not healthful. I did not want my child eating almost nothing but high-sugar, low-nutrient foods. If anything, my desire for my child to eat a healthy diet was even stronger than it had been prior to his birth.

Bradley has a congenital heart defect. A heart-healthy diet with plenty of whole plant foods would be very important for his long-term health. He had already been receiving a healthy, nutritious diet of pureed food through his feeding tube. Did I truly need to throw my hands into the air and give up on this dream of that same diet being eaten by him orally? I decided the answer was no.

It turns out that I was correct. Three months after his therapy began at the clinic, Bradley began eating small amounts of pureed, nutritious food. The following 7 months were full of many ups and downs and periods of tremendous strides and total regression.

And then, finally, Bradley was eating all of his food by mouth, receiving only liquid through his tube. Later, Bradley was drinking everything but his water. The day finally came, when Bradley was 4 years old, in which he consumed all food and liquids orally. He no longer needed his feeding tube, and he became tube free for the first time in his life.

Even better, Bradley was eating a variety of healthful, nutrient-rich foods. The only catch was that these foods had to be in a very smooth puree. He was not yet ready for solid food. Any solid particle in his food lead to immediate gagging and vomiting.

In time, that changed. But, for a solid year, I learned to pack as much nutrition into a small volume of pureed food as possible. Every day, he proves to the world that kids with oral aversion do not by default have to resort high-sugar, low-nutrient food to become able to eat.

* * *

THERE ARE a variety of reasons a child requires a pureed diet. Some children are unable to swallow solid food due to a swallowing disorder, but are able to swallow pureed food. Like Bradley, some children have sensory disorders that prevent them from being able to consume solid food. Whatever the case, the goal should be to include as many nutritious foods as is possible.

How many foods that will be will vary from child to child. I will add that many adults have swallowing disorders as well, and these adults should not be forced to give up good food as a result. Adults with swallowing disorders can and should be able to consume healthful, delicious food just like everyone else.

In this book, you will find 100 recipes for pureed food. I have provided recipes that suit a variety of needs, including dairy free, gluten free, soy free, vegan, and vegetarian recipes so there should be plenty for most people in spite of dietary restrictions. For the most part, recipes contain inexpensive ingredients. Overall, I believe you will be quite surprised with how affordable a diet of real food can be.

I believe in the power of real food, and the more real food that goes into a child's body, the better that child's body will be able to function.

WHY BOTHER?

THE MOTHER of a tube-fed child shared a story with me not too long ago. She feeds a diet of pureed food through her son's feeding tube. She purees real food in a high powered blender and feeds it through her child's feeding tube. She does not use enteral formula. This is exactly how I fed Bradley after the age of 1 when he was 100% tube-fed.

This mother's son was in the hospital, and she discussed his diet with the hospital staff. After explaining what she feeds her child, one of the doctors looked at her and asked, "Why bother with doing all of this? Just feed him formula."

I have heard many stories similar to this. I have never understood these kinds of questions. I assume that same doctor doesn't feed his own children nothing but formula, but instead, feeds them food in spite of the extra effort doing so requires.

The implication is that children with feeding tubes or feeding disorders are simply not worth the same amount of time and effort as children without feeding tubes and feeding disorders. For most people, a diet of nothing but formula is not appropriate over the age of 1. These diets defy the dietary recommendations of virtually every major medical, health, and dietary organization in the entire world.

The American Dietetic Association, for example, recommends that most vitamins and minerals be consumed through natural foods, not through synthetic supplements. Yet, enteral formula, Pediasure ™, and other formulas contains only synthetic vitamins and minerals. They contain no natural foods at all.

Plant foods contain phytonutrients, which are vital to experiencing the most optimal health possible over the long term. Yet, these formulas contain no phytonutrients whatsoever. A child living entirely off these formulas will consume no phytonutrients at all.

The World Health Organization, The American Medical Association, the American Heart Association, and more all recommend that both children and adults consume carbohydrates largely from whole grains, fruits, and vegetables while limiting carbohydrates from sugars. Yet, the formulas pushed onto parents of children with feeding disorders provide almost all carbohydrates from sugars.

Why do these formulas continue to be recommended by the very people belonging to organizations that stand against these kinds of diets? There seems to be some sort of disconnect that has happened. One problem is that the one and only variable used to measure the effectiveness of these formulas is weight gain and growth. It is assumed that if a child is growing and gaining weight appropriately, the child is being fed a healthful diet. But, this simply is not true.

There are so many more variables involved in determining a child's health, especially their long-term health than whether they are gaining weight. There are absolutely no long-term studies of the health outcomes of children consuming these formulas in large quantities. And shame on the medical profession for recommending these products in spite of this lack of data.

Surely, the average medical professional is aware that the negative effects of a diet can take a long time to show up. A 20-year-old eating a high sodium diet will not suddenly die of a heart attack a few months after beginning such a diet. However, the cardiovascular health of that individual will indeed be affected more and more, little by little, as time passes. These formulas have not been appropriately studied and therefore, should be recommended only with extreme hesitation.

Meanwhile, we do know that diets full of natural foods lead to more positive health outcomes. There is an abundance of long-term studies that show us this is true. Diets rich in fruits, vegetables, and whole grains lead to a decreased risk of every major, chronic illness in existence.

So, why bother, you ask? Because my son's health is important to me. It is a very high priority in my life. In spite of my son's feeding disorder, he is absolutely worth the effort just like other children are worth the effort of preparing and feeding real food.

THE HOW OF FEEDING NUTRITIOUS FOOD

For mothers and fathers of children with feeding disorders, imagining their children eating diets of healthful foods can seem very daunting, if not impossible. I am certainly not suggesting that transitioning to a diet of real food will be an easy journey. On the contrary, I am sure it will not be simple. Some children will transition surprisingly quickly. Others will require weeks, months, or even years.

The point is to get as much real food into your child's body as possible. If that means only a small amount in the beginning, that's ok. Just keep working at it. Keep believing and don't give up. Make extremely tiny changes at a time if you need to. If it doesn't work, keep offering these foods again and again. Some children need a long time to become familiar enough with a new food to feel safe eating it. So, keep working at it.

If your child is one that must transition extremely slowly, try some of these recipes and freeze them into half-sized ice cubes. Thaw out one cube each day and allow your child to explore it in the way he/she feels comfortable. At first, there may be no exploring of the food. That's ok. Keep offering it. The advantage of freezing in such small quantities is that you will not be wasting large quantities of food as you move through this process.

In time, your child will eventually move toward exploring the food and then, eating the food. This process can happen over a period of days, or it can take an extremely long time. Allow your child to lead the way. Keep offering the food. When it seems to be going terribly, keep offering the food. When you feel things will never improve, keep offering the food. Keep offering the food. This will be a hardcore exercise in patience.

If your child is just now beginning treatment of oral aversion and has been fed through a feeding tube, it is my opinion that real, nutritious food should be given from the very beginning. By starting out this way, these are the foods your child will become familiar with and eventually, feel safe with. It may be that offering lots of sweets will move the process along a little more quickly. For me, I did not care.

My goal was for my child to become able to eat a reasonable diet, not to be rid of the feeding tube absolutely as soon as possible through any means. I also recommend, whenever possible, to feed a blenderized diet through your child's feeding tube. I would not be surprised if the reason many tube-fed children struggle to transition to real food is because their body is never fed real food.

Their body is used to enteral formula, so real food is not only shocking to the mouth, but to the entire digestive system as a whole. I do believe feeding Bradley a diet of real food through his feeding tube was a huge, contributing factor to his success of weaning off of his feeding tube onto a diet of nutritious food.

If you would like more information about blenderized diets, please visit my blog at crunchytubiemama.com. In fact, all of these recipes can be fed through a feeding tube if pureed in a high-powered blender. For some children that are partially eating pureed food orally and partially eating through their feeding tube, an option may be to offer the food you would like your child to eat for a meal, allow your child to eat what he/she is able, and then, feed the remaining portion through the feeding tube. Always speak to your child's medical team about any dietary changes.

And so, here we are. The only equipment you need to feed your child a pureed diet is a blender. You will find that a high-powered blender, such as a Vitamix or Blendtec will greatly increase the variety of foods you are able to feed your child. Lower level blenders often require more liquid to properly puree, which can increase volume. This can be a problem for many children.

At the time of this writing, both Vitamix and Blendtec offer a medical discount for families with a member who requires a pureed diet. Otherwise, the only other item you need is food. As you become more familiar with my recipes, I hope you will branch out and invent some of your own!

Each recipe is labeled to help you identify which recipes are suitable for a variety of dietary restrictions. They are labeled with the following abbreviations:

DF = DAIRY FREE

SF = SOY FREE

GF = GLUTEN FREE

V = VEGAN

VG = VEGETARIAN

SOME FOODS TEND to thicken as they sit. For this reason, many of the recipes contain as little liquid as possible to move the purees in a high-powered blender. You may need to add a little water if the food is not pureeing well in the blender, but use only just enough to get the food moving around in the blender properly. If you find the puree to be too thick just prior to serving, add some liquid to thin.

In most cases, recipes include several servings so that they can be frozen and simply thawed and served. This makes it possible to prepare food once per week or even once per month if necessary. However, some recipes include ingredients that cannot be safely frozen, so a smaller number of servings are included along with a warning to not freeze.

Always keep in mind that pureed food spoils more quickly than non-pureed food. So, while your plate of food may remain safe in the refrigerator for 4-5 days, the same cannot be said of pureed food containing identical ingredients as your plate of food. Most pureed food will remain safe for consumption for 48 hours in the refrigerator.

The recommendation is 48-72 hours, but since I do not have a laboratory to test my son's food to determine exactly when it goes bad, I stick with the lower end of that range. For the immunocompromised, I recommend and even more stringent standard, discarding any pureed food that has been refrigerated for more than 24 hours.

Each recipe provides an estimation of the calories, carbohydrates, fat, and protein for each serving. This information was calculated using the particular brands I use or the USDA Nutrition Database. When brands may substantially impact the calories present in a recipe, I have broken down the nutritional information of each ingredient. This way, if you need to substitute for a different brand, you can subtract the nutritional information from my preferred brand, and add in the nutritional information of your preferred brand.

When cooking vegetables, you can buy frozen that steam in the microwave or purchase them fresh and sauté them, steam them in a steamer, or however else you prefer to cook them.

The totals of calories and macronutrients are for the entire recipe as a whole. This is because serving sizes will vary from person to person. Divide the recipe into the number of servings you need and then, divide the nutritional information of the total batch by the number of servings.

For example, if you a recipe makes 8 servings, divide the nutrition total by 8 to calculate the per serving nutritional information. I have included recipes for low-volume calorie boosters you can then add if you need to increase the number of calories per serving.

IMPORTANT NOTE: I do not list the volume created by these recipes. This is because volume will vary from family to family. Which blender you use, the amount of liquid in the particular foods you have purchased and more impact the volume of the final outcome. You may need to change the amount of liquid used in these recipes because of the variables. Blending is an art, not a science. Diets do not require precision, and this is all ok.

It is best to blend the recipe, divide the batch into servings that are the volume you need per serving, and then, add a calorie booster if needed. Keep a notebook as you make recipes, and take notes about any changes you made to suit your particular needs.

ENTREES

BLUEBERRY CHICKPEA MASH

DF*, SF, GF, VG
Ingredients:

- 1 cup blueberries
- 1 cup canned chickpeas, rinsed and drained
- 1/4 cup heavy cream*
- 2-3 rosemary leaves
- 1/4 cup honey

*For dairy free, substitute the cream with cashew cream from the boosters section

Blueberry Chickpea Mash	Calories	Carbohydrates	Fat	Protein
Blueberries	84	28	0	0
Chickpeas	268	44	4	12
Heavy cream	200	0	24	0
Rosemary leaves	Negligible			
Honey	240	68	0	0
Total	792	140	28	12

CINNA-BEANS

DF, SF, GF, V, VG

- 1 cup cannellini beans
- 1 cup sweet potatoes, peeled and baked
- 1/2 Tbsp cinnamon
- 1/8 tsp nutmeg

Cinna-Beans	Calories	Carbohydrates	Fat	Protein
Cannelini beans	308	55	0	22
Sweet potatoes	170	39	0	3
Cinnamon	Negligible	0	0	0
Nutmeg	Negligible	0	0	0
Total	478	94	0	25

SARDINE SMASH

SF, GF

- 1 can sardines*
- 3 oz cream cheese
- 1/4 cup tomato sauce

*Always check the ingredient and nutrition labels of sardines. Choose sardines lower in sodium and without oils such as soy, vegetable, or canola oil.

DO NOT FREEZE. Sardines become rancid when frozen. Blend and use within 48 hours.

Sardine Smash	Calories	Carbohydrates	Fat	Protein
Sardines	190	0	11	24
Cream cheese	270	6	27	6
Tomato sauce	20	4	0	0
Total	480	10	38	30

HOORAY! PB & J

DF, SF, GF*, VG

- 10 strawberries
- 3 pieces whole grain bread
- 2 Tbsp chia seeds
- 1/4 cup honey
- 2 Tbsp natural peanut butter

*For gluten free, use gluten free bread

Hooray! PB&J	Calories	Carbohydrates	Fat	Protein
Strawberries	38	9	0	1
Bread	120	33	0	9
Chia seeds	160	12	10	6
Honey	240	68	0	0
Peanut butter	200	7	17	8
Total	758	129	27	24

BLUEBERRY MUFFINS

DF, SF, GF*, V, VG

- 2 cups blueberries
- 8 pieces bread
- 2/3 cup maple syrup
- 1/3 cup olive oil
- 2/3 cup peanut butter
- 2 cups milk or dairy alternative

*For gluten free, use gluten free bread

Blueberry muffins	Calories	Carbohydrates	Fat	Protein
Blueberries	168	56	0	0
Bread	880	160	20	16
Maple syrup	586	144	0	0
Olive oil	666	0	75	0
Peanut butter	1066	37	90	42
Milk	320	26	16	16
Total	3686	423	201	74

GARLIC VEGGIE PASTA

DF, SF, GF*, V, VG

- 4 cups whole grain pasta, prepared
- 4 1/2 cups cooked broccoli
- 1 1/2 cups water
- 5 garlic cloves, roasted**
- 1/2 cup olive oil

*For GF, use gluten free pasta
**See misc section

Garlic Veggie Pasta	Calories	Carbohydrates	Fat	Protein
Pasta	480	104	1	3
Broccoli	105	14	0	7
Water	0	0	0	0
Garlic cloves	Negligible			
Olive oil	480		56	
Total	1065	118	57	10

CHEESEBURGER

SF, GF*

- 1 pound 85% lean ground beef, cooked
- 8 oz block cheddar cheese
- 8 oz can tomato sauce
- 1/4 cup mustard
- 1/4 cup dill relish
- 4 slices whole grain bread
- 2 cups milk

*For gluten free, use gluten free bread

Cheeseburger	Calories	Carbohydrates	Fat	Protein
Beef	960	0	68	84
Cheese	880	0	72	56
Tomato sauce	70	14	0	0
Mustard	Negligible			
Dill relish	Negligible			
Bread	400	80	4	12
Milk	320	26	16	16
Total	2630	120	160	168

FISH STICKS

DF, SF, GF*

- 4 tilapia fillets, baked
- 2 slices whole grain bread
- 1/2 cup mayonnaise
- 1 Tbsp dill relish
- 1 Tbsp mustard

*For gluten free, use gluten free bread

To bake tilapia fillets, place on baking sheet lined with parchment paper, and bake at 400 degrees for 10-12 minutes.

Fish Sticks	Calories	Carbohydrates	Fat	Protein
Tilapia filets	360	8	8	68
Bread	200	40	2	6
Mayonnaise	720	0	72	0
Relish	Negligible			
Mustard	Negligible			
Total	1280	48	82	74

GRILLED CHEESE

SF, GF*, VG

- 8 slices whole grain bread
- 8 oz block cheddar cheese
- 4 Tbsp butter, melted
- 2 1/2 cups milk

*For gluten free, use gluten free bread

Prior to blending, brush the bread with the melted butter, and bake at 400 degrees for 10-15 minutes.

Grilled Cheese	Calories	Carbohydrates	Fat	Protein
Bread	800	160	8	24
Cheese	880	0	72	56
Butter	400	0	44	0
Milk	400	32	20	20
Total	2480	192	144	100

SPAGHETTI

DF, SF, GF*

- 1 15.5 oz can tomato sauce
- 4 basil leaves
- 1/2 Tbsp oregano
- 1/2 pound 85% lean hamburger, cooked
- 1/2 pound whole grain spaghetti noodles, prepared**

*For gluten free, use gluten free noodles
**Weight is prior to preparation

Spaghetti	Calories	Carbohydrates	Fat	Protein
Tomato sauce	122	24	0	8
Basil leaves	Negligible			
Oregano	Negligible			
Hamburger	480	0	34	42
Noodles	720	156	6	48
Total	1322	180	40	98

OMELETTE & TOAST

DF*, SF, GF**, VG

- 4 slices whole grain bread
- 4 eggs, fried
- 4 oz block cheddar cheese
- 2 cups milk

*For dairy free, use dairy alternative
**For gluten free, use gluten free bread

Omelette and toast	Calories	Carbohydrates	Fat	Protein
Bread	400	80	4	12
Eggs	286	1	19	25
Cheddar cheese	440	0	36	28
Milk	320	25	16	16
Total	1446	106	75	81

DAIRY FREE MAC 'N' CHEEZE

DF, SF, GF*, V, VG

- 1 medium eggplant, peeled, sliced, and baked
- 4 cups whole grain pasta, prepared
- 1 cup onion, chopped and sautéed
- 1/2 cup dairy alternative
- 1/2 cup nutritional yeast
- 2 roasted garlic cloves**

*For GF, use gluten free pasta
**See misc section
To bake eggplant, peel and slice it, place slices on a baking sheet lines with parchment paper, and bake at 400 degrees for 25 minutes.

Dairy Free Mac n Cheese	Calories	Carbohydrates	Fat	Protein
Eggplant	114	27	1	4
Pasta	480	104	1	3
Onion	23	5	0	0
Dairy alternative	40	0	2	4
Nutritional yeast	120	10	1	16
Garlic cloves	Negligible			
Total	777	146	5	27

ROAST BEEF SANDWICHES

DF*, SF, GF**

- 1 roasted garlic clove
- 2/3 cup olive oil
- 1/4 cup white vinegar
- 1/4 cup apple cider vinegar
- 1/4 cup honey
- 1 tsp worcestershire sauce
- 1 tsp dijon mustard
- 1 tsp paprika
- 3/4 tsp salt
- 1/2 tsp garlic powder
- 1/2 tsp onion powder
- 3 pounds pork butt roast, roasted
- 2 onions, chopped
- 12 romaine lettuce leaves
- 6 roma tomatoes
- 6 slices bread
- 2 cups milk

You will likely need to blend in two separate batches and combine in a large mixing bowl before portioning into serving sizes.

*For dairy free, use dairy alternative

**For gluten free, use gluten free bread

Roast the pork (fat side up) and onions in roasting pan filled with a cup of water at 300 degrees for 25 minutes per pound or until the center reaches 180 degrees F.

Roast Beef Sandwiches	Calories	Carbohydrates	Fat	Protein
Garlic	Negligible			
Olive oil	633	0	74	0
White vinegar	Negligible			
Apple cider vinegar	Negligible			
Honey	240	68	0	0
Worcestershire sauce	Negligible			
Mustard	Negligible			
Paprika	Negligible			
Salt	Negligible			
Garlic powder	Negligible			
Onion powder	Negligible			
Pork	2527	0	156	252
Onions	44	10	0	1
Lettuce	Negligible			
Tomatoes	213	2	3	6
Bread	600	120	6	18
Milk	320	26	16	16
Total	4577	226	255	293

TOM KHA SOUP

DF, GF, V, VG

- 1 inch ginger, peeled
- 2 Tbsp lemon zest
- 2 Tbsp honey
- 1 tsp lime zest
- 2 cans full fat coconut milk
- 2 cups water
- 2 Tbsp low sodium soy sauce
- 1/4 tsp salt
- 1 block tofu (firm), chopped
- 1/4 cup cilantro

Place all ingredients into a large sauce pan and simmer for 25 minutes. Cool and blend.

TOM KHA SOUP

Tom Kha Soup	Calories	Carbohydrates	Fat	Protein
Ginger	Negligible			
Lemon zest	Negligible			
Honey	120	34	0	0
Lime zest	Negligible			
Coconut milk	1500	20	150	20
Water	0	0	0	0
Soy sauce	Negligible			
Salt	0	0	0	0
Tofu	350	10	18	35
Cilantro	Negligible			
Total	1970	64	168	55

MAC 'N' CHEESE

SF, GF*, VG

- 4 cups whole grain pasta
- 8 oz block cheddar cheese
- 3/4 cup heavy cream

*For gluten free, use gluten free pasta

Mac 'n' Cheese	Calories	Carbohydrates	Fat	Protein
Pasta	480	104	1	3
Cheese	880	0	72	56
3/4 cup heavy cream	600	12	60	0
Total	1960	116	133	59

PIZZA PASTA

SF, GF*, VG

- 4 cups whole grain pasta
- 1 cup pizza sauce
- 1/2 cup heavy cream
- 8 oz block cheddar cheese

*For gluten free, use gluten free pasta

Pizza Pasta	Calories	Carbohydrates	Fat	Protein
Pasta	480	104	1	3
Pizza sauce	35	7	1	1
Heavy Cream	400	0	48	0
Cheese	880	0	72	56
Total	1795	111	122	60

CHICKEN POT PIE

DF, SF, GF*

- 2 medium potatoes, baked
- 1 bag baby carrots, baked
- 3 chicken drumsticks, skin on, bone discarded
- 2 1/2 cups low-sodium chicken broth
- 1 pie crust, prepared according to package directions

*For gluten free, use gluten free pie crust

Roast potatoes, carrots and drumsticks prior to blending. Potatoes and carrots can also be chopped and boiled until soft instead, if desired.

Alternatively, the drumsticks (with bones) can be simmered for 4-12 hours in water to create broth, which can be used in this recipe. Remove skin and meat for blending.

Chicken Pot Pie	Calories	Carbohydrates	Fat	Protein
Potatoes	336	74	0	8
Carrots	187	43	4	5
Chicken	601	0	31	73
Broth	0	0	0	0
Pie crust	760	96	40	0
Total	1884	213	75	86

RANCH CHICKEN NUGGETS

SF, GF

- 5 chicken drumsticks, skin on, bone discarded
- 1 cup low-sodium chicken broth
- 4 pieces bread
- 2/3 cup full fat plain yogurt
- 2 Tbsp ranch powder**

*For gluten free, use gluten free bread
**See recipe in Misc chapter

Roast drumsticks prior to blending. Alternatively, the drumsticks (with bones) can be simmered for 4-12 hours in water to create broth, which can be used in this recipe. Remove skin and meat for blending.

RANCH CHICKEN NUGGETS

Ranch chicken nuggets	Calories	Carbohydrates	Fat	Protein
Chicken drumsticks	1003	0	53	122
Broth	0	0	0	0
Bread	400	80	4	12
Yogurt	150	7	5	5
Ranch powder	26	4	0	1
Total	1579	91	62	140

BBQ CHICKEN NUGGETS

DF, SF, GF*

- 5 chicken drumsticks, skin one, bone discarded
- 1 cup low-sodium chicken broth
- 4 pieces bread
- 2/3 cup natural BBQ sauce

*For gluten free, use gluten free bread

Roast drumsticks prior to blending. Alternatively, the drumsticks (with bones) can be simmered for 4-12 hours in water to create broth, which can be used in this recipe. Remove skin and meat for blending.

BBQ chicken nuggets	Calories	Carbohydrates	Fat	Protein
Chicken drumsticks	1003	0	53	122
Broth	0	0	0	0
Bread	400	80	4	12
BBQ sauce	186	48		5
Total	1589	128	57	139

SALAD

DF*, SF, GF, V, VG

- 4 cups baby spinach
- 2 cups sliced mushrooms, raw
- 5 roma tomatoes
- 2 cups garbanzo beans
- 1/2 cucumber
- 14 baby carrots
- 1 cup dressing**

*For dairy free, choose dairy free dressing
**See misc section

Salad	Calories	Carbohydrates	Fat	Protein
Baby spinach	26	4	0	2
Mushrooms	31	4	0	4
Tomatoes	72	16	0	4
Garbanzo beans	420	90	7	21
Cucumber	23	5	0	1
Carrots	52	12	0	1
Dressing	598	18	58	9
Total	1222	149	65	42

NO COOK FRENCH TOAST

DF*, SF, GF**, V*, VG

- 7 slices bread
- 1 cup milk
- 1/4 tsp nutmeg
- 1/2 tsp cinnamon
- 1/2 tsp vanilla
- 1/4 cup maple syrup

*For dairy free and vegan, use dairy alternative
**For gluten free, use gluten free bread

No Cook French Toast	Calories	Carbohydrates	Fat	Protein
7 slices bread	700	140	7	21
1 cup milk	160	12	8	8
1/4 tsp nutmeg	Negligible			
1/2 tsp cinnamon	Negligible			
1/2 tsp vanilla	Negligible			
1/4 cup maple syrup	220	48	0	
Total	1080	200	15	29

SLOPPY JOES

DF, SF, GF*

- 1 pound 85% lean ground beef, cooked
- 4 slices bread
- 2 cloves roasted garlic**
- 1 15.5 oz can tomato sauce
- 2 Tbsp white vinegar
- 1 onion, chopped (cook with ground beef)
- 1/4 cup honey
- 1 Tbsp molasses
- 1/2 tsp salt
- 2 Tbsp worcestershire sauce
- 1 tsp mustard
- 1 tsp garlic powder
- 1/4 cup dill relish

*For gluten free, use gluten free bread
**See misc section

SLOPPY JOES

Sloppy Joes	Calories	Carbohydrates	Fat	Protein
1 pound ground beef	960	0	68	84
4 slices bread	400	80	4	12
2 gloves garlic	Negligible			
2 cups (16 oz) cups tomato sauce	122	24	0	8
2 Tbsp white vinegar	Negligible			
1 onion, chopped	23	5	0	0
1/4 cup honey/maple syrup	240	68	0	0
1 Tbsp molasses	60	14	0	1
.5 tsp salt	Negligible			
2 Tbsp worcestershire sauce	Negligible			
1 tsp mustard	Negligible			
1 tsp garlic powder	Negligible			
1/4 cup dill relish	Negligible			
Total	1805	191	72	105

NACHOS

SF, GF

- 1 large tomato
- 8 oz block cheddar cheese
- 1/2 pound 85% lean ground beef, cooked
- Pinch chili powder
- 6 corn tortillas
- 1/2 cup milk

Nachos	Calories	Carbohydrates	Fat	Protein
Tomato	33	7	0	1
Cheese	880	0	72	56
Ground beef	480	0	34	42
Chili powder	Negligible			
Corn tortillas	361	78	3	6
Milk	80	6	2	4
Total	1834	91	111	109

LASAGNA

SF, GF*

- 1 15.5 oz can tomato sauce
- 4 basil leaves
- 1/2 Tbsp oregano
- 1/2 pound 85% lean ground beef, cooked
- 1/2 pound whole grain spaghetti noodles, prepared**
- 1 cup cottage cheese
- 4 oz block cheddar cheese
- 1 cup water

*For GF, use gluten free noodles
**Weight is prior to preparation

Lasagna	Calories	Carbohydrates	Fat	Protein
Tomato sauce	122	24	0	8
Basil leaves	Negligible			
Oregano	Negligible			
Ground Beef	480	0	34	42
Noodles	720	156	6	48
Cottage cheese	181	12	3	24
Cheese	440	0	36	28
1 cup water	0	0	0	0
Total	1943	192	79	150

DAIRY FREE NACHOS

DF, SF, GF

- 1 large tomato
- 1/2 cup nutritional yeast
- 1/2 pound 85% lean ground beef, cooked
- Pinch chili powder
- 6 corn tortillas
- 1/2 cup dairy alternative

Dairy Free Nachos	Calories	Carbohydrates	Fat	Protein
Tomato	33	7	0	1
Nutritional yeast	120	10	1	16
Ground beef	480	0	34	42
Chili powder	Negligible			
Corn tortillas	361	78	3	6
Dairy alternative	40	0	2	4
Total	1034	95	40	69

CHILI MAC

SF, GF*

- 1 pound 85% lean ground beef, cooked
- 1 can kidney beans, drained and rinsed
- 1 cup onion, chopped (cook with ground beef)
- 3 cloves roasted garlic**
- 14 oz can diced tomatoes
- 15.5 oz can tomato sauce
- 2 Tbsp chili powder
- 1 tsp cumin
- 4 cups whole grain pasta
- 8 oz block cheddar cheese

*For gluten free, use gluten free pasta
**See misc section

Chili Mac	Calories	Carbohydrates	Fat	Protein
Ground beef	960	0	68	84
Kidney beans	385	70	0	25
Onion, chopped	23	5	0	0
Garlic cloves	Negligible			
Tomatoes	112	21	0	3
Tomato sauce	122	24	0	8
Chili powder	Negligible			
Cumin	Negligible			
Pasta	480	104	1	3
Cheese	880	0	72	56
Total	2962	224	141	179

PASTA W/ WHITE SAUCE

DF, GF*, V, VG

- 1 block tofu (firm)
- 2 cups dairy alternative
- 1 Tbsp oregano
- 1 leaf sage
- 1/4 cup olive oil
- 1 tsp salt
- 1/4 cup nutritional yeast
- Juice from half lemon
- 1 clove roasted garlic**
- 4 cups whole grain pasta, prepared

*For gluten free, use gluten free pasta
**See misc section

PASTA W/ WHITE SAUCE

Pasta w/ white sauce	Calories	Carbohydrates	Fat	Protein
Tofu	350	10	18	35
Dairy alternative	160	0	8	16
Oregano	Negligible			
Sage	Negligible			
Olive oil	480	0	56	0
1 tsp salt	Negligible			
Nutritional yeast	60	5	1	8
Lemon Juice	Negligible			
Garlic	Negligible			
Pasta	480	104	1	3
Total	1530	119	84	62

EGG-LESS SCRAMBLED EGGS

DF, GF, V, VG

- 2 blocks tofu (firm), chopped
- 2 cups dairy alternative
- 1/4 cup nutritional yeast
- 1 clove roasted garlic*
- 4 cups baby spinach
- 1 cup onion, chopped
- 1/2 tsp cumin
- 1 1/2 tsp turmeric
- 1 tsp paprika
- 1/4 cup olive oil

*See misc section

Add all ingredients to a large skillet and simmer in 2 cups water until water is evaporated. Cool and blend.

EGG-LESS SCRAMBLED EGGS

Egg-less scrambled eggs	Calories	Carbohydrates	Fat	Protein
Tofu	700	20	36	70
Dairy alternative	160	0	8	16
Nutritional yeast	60	5	1	8
Garlic	Negligible			
Baby spinach	26	4	0	2
Onion	23	5	0	0
Cumin	Negligible			
Turmeric	Negligible			
Paprika	Negligible			
Olive oil	480	0	56	0
Total	1449	34	101	96

CEREALS

This chapter lists recipes for cooking plain grains. These grains are handy to freeze into ice cubes. When you need a carbohydrate or fiber boost, just thaw 1-2 cubes out and mix them into a puree.

They can also be used for a blender-free quick meal by thawing and heating the amount you desire and stirring a little olive oil, honey, and milk or dairy alternative. Or, blend the same ingredients just mentioned with some fruit in the blender.

There are many ways to use these grains, so they are handy to keep around. I kept a large container in the freezer with a variety of grain cubes and found them useful on a regular basis.

Even better, they are very quick to make. Just mix the water and grain together in a saucepan, and simmer until soft. Pour into the blender with any needed additional water and then, pour into an ice cube tray for freezing. Count the number of ice cubes and divide the total nutritional content by the number of cubes to determine the nutritional content of each cube.

Amaranth

1/2 cup amaranth
1 3/4 cups water

- Calories: 358
- Carbohydrates: 63
- Fat: 6
- Protein: 13

Barley

2 cups barley
1 cup water

- Calories: 1408
- Carbohydrates: 310
- Fat: 5
- Protein: 40

Brown Rice

2 cups brown rice
1 1/2 cups water

- Calories: 400
- Carbohydrates: 85
- Fat: 3
- Protein: 8

Bulgur

1 cup bulgur
2 cups water

- Calories: 479
- Carbohydrates: 106
- Fat: 2
- Protein: 17

Cornmeal Mush

1 cup cornmeal
2 cups water

- Calories: 442
- Carbohydrates: 94
- Fat: 4
- Protein: 10

Farro

1 1/2 cups farro
2 cups water

- Calories: 560
- Carbohydrates: 120
- Fat: 0
- Protein: 24

Freekeh

1 cup freekeh
4 cups water

- Calories: 520
- Carbohydrates: 140
- Fat: 4
- Protein: 32

Millet

1 cup millet
1 1/2 cups water

- Calories: 756
- Carbohydrates: 145
- Fat: 8
- Protein: 22

Oatmeal

1 1/2 cups oatmeal
2 1/2 cups water

- Calories: 450
- Carbohydrates: 84
- Fat: 7
- Protein: 15

Quinoa

1 cup quinoa
2 1/2 cups water

- Calories: 626
- Carbohydrates: 109
- Fat: 10
- Protein: 24

*Quinoa can have a rather bitter taste to it due to a waxy coating on the outside of each grain. To remove this coating, pour the quinoa into a fine sieve and move it around in the sieve while running water over it for 1-2 minutes. Continue with preparation from there.

Sorghum

1 cup sorghum
3 cups water

- Calories: 632
- Carbohydrates: 138
- Fat: 6
- Protein: 20

*Soak sorghum overnight in 4 cups water. Drain and rinse. Continue with preparation from there.

Spelt

1/2 cup spelt
2 1/2 cups water

- Calories: 294
- Carbohydrates: 61
- Fat: 2
- Protein: 13

*Before cooking the spelt, run it through a dry blender to grind it.

Teff
1 cup teff
3 cups water

- Calories: 708
- Carbohydrates: 141
- Fat: 5
- Protein: 26

Wheat
1 cup whole wheat flour
2 1/2 cups water

- Calories: 495
- Carbohydrates: 100
- Fat: 2
- Protein: 16

Wild Rice
1 1/3 cup wild rice
3 cups water

- Calories: 760
- Carbohydrates: 160
- Fat: 2
- Protein: 31

FRUITS AND VEGGIES

ADD WATER, milk, or dairy alternative for blending as you choose. Start very small and add more as needed. How much is necessary depends on how much water is in your fruits and veggies, which will vary.

MANGO TANGO

DF, SF, GF, V, VG

- 1 Apple
- 3 Large carrots, boiled until soft
- 1 mango, peeled and pit removed*

Calories: 327
Carbohydrates: 92
Fat: 1
Protein: 4

*While mango can be a nutritious part of a healthful diet, it is quite high in fructose compared to other options. While the higher calories of this recipe may be tempt you to use it daily, I do recommend it be used in moderation.

SQUASHED BEANS

DF, SF, GF, V, VG

- 2 cups summer squash, cooked
- 2 cups green beans, cooked
- 1 garlic clove

Calories: 150
Carbohydrates: 29
Fat: 1
Protein: 7

ORANGE CARROT

DF, SF, GF, VG

- 6 medium oranges, peeled and de-seeded
- 6 cups carrots, cooked
- 1/4 cup honey

Calories: 959
Carbohydrates: 230
Fat: 1
Protein: 7

SWEET POTATO SQUASH

DF, SF, GF, V, VG

- 3 sweet potatoes, baked
- 1 medium squash, baked

Calories: 342
Carbohydrates: 76
Fat: 1
Protein: 8

BANANA BLUEBERRY

DF, SF, GF, V, VG

- 3 bananas
- 2 cups blueberries
- 1 tsp cinnamon

Calories: 484
Carbohydrates: 123
Fat: 2
Protein: 6

PEACHY PEAS

DF, SF, GF, V, VG

- 2 cups peas, cooked
- 4 peaches, peeled and seed removed

Calories: 411
Carbohydrates: 85
Fat: 2
Protein: 19

CALIFORNIA BLEND

DF, SF, GF, V, VG

- 1 cup cauliflower, cooked
- 1 cup carrots, cooked
- 1 cup broccoli, cooked
- 1 Tbsp oregano

Calories: 133
Carbohydrates: 26
Fat: 0
Protein: 8

PRUNES

DF, SF, GF, V, VG

- 16 prunes
- 3 cups water

Calories: 440
Carbohydrates: 104
Fat: 0
Protein: 4

BEET-A-LICIOUS

DF, SF, GF, V, VG

- 3 bananas
- 1 cup cherries, seed removed
- 1/2 can beets*

*Always read ingredients to be sure you are only purchasing beets. Some canned beets contain high fructose corn syrup and other ingredients that are best avoided.

Calories: 472
   Carbohydrates: 344
   Fat: 1
   Protein: 6

POTINI

DF, SF, GF, V, VG

- 1 cup zucchini, cooked
- 1 sweet potato, baked
- 1 cup mushrooms, cooked
- 1 tsp thyme

Calories: 138
Carbohydrates: 29
Fat: 0
Protein: 5

CARROTS 'N' BRUSSELS

DF, SF, GF, VG

- 4 cups Brussels sprouts, cooked
- 2 cups carrots, cooked
- 1/4 tsp nutmeg
- 2 Tbsp honey

Calories: 391
Carbohydrates: 89
Fat: 1
Protein: 16

CUCUMBER SALAD

DF, SF, GF, VG

- 4 medium tomatoes
- 2 medium cucumbers
- 1/4 red onion
- 1/2 cup rice vinegar
- 1 Tbsp honey
- 1 Tbsp fresh dill, chopped
- 1/2 tsp salt

Calories: 250
Carbohydrates: 60
Fat: 1
Protein: 4

SWEET, SWEET CAULIFLOWER

DF, SF, GF, V, VG

- 3 sweet potatoes, baked
- 1 medium cauliflower, cooked

Calories: 455
Carbohydrates: 100
Fat: 1
Protein: 18

CREAMED SPINACH

SF, GF, VG

- 5 cups spinach, cooked*
- 8 oz cream cheese
- 4 Tbsp butter

*Measure BEFORE cooking

Calories: 1143
  Carbohydrates: 20
  Fat: 116
  Protein: 19

SQUASHINI

DF, SF, GF, V, VG

- 3 medium zucchini, cooked
- 3 summer squash, cooked

Calories: 202
Carbohydrates: 36
Fat: 0
Protein: 10

BEANS 'N' PEARS

DF, SF, GF, V, VG

- 2 cups green beans, cooked
- 2 pears, cored

Calories: 285
Carbohydrates: 70
Fat: 0
Protein: 5

PEAS AND CARROTS

DF, SF, GF, V, VG

- 2 cups peas, cooked
- 2 cups carrots, cooked

Calories: 355
Carbohydrates: 66
Fat: 1
Protein: 19

SPIN-APP-ANA

DF, SF, GF, V, VG

- 1 cup baby spinach
- 1 banana
- 2 apples
- 1 cup strawberries

Calories: 347
Carbohydrates: 88
Fat: 0
Protein: 3

BEETBERRIES

DF, SF, GF, V, VG

- 1/2 can beets*
- 1 cup blueberries

*Always read ingredients to be sure you are only purchasing beets. Some canned beets contain high fructose corn syrup and other ingredients that are best avoided.

Calories: 144
　　Carbohydrates: 35
　　Fat: 0
　　Protein: 2

PUMPKINANA

DF, SF, GF, V, VG

- 1/2 cup pumpkin puree
- 2 apples, cored
- 1 banana
- 1/4 tsp nutmeg

Calories: 334
Carbohydrates: 86
Fat: 0
Protein: 4

PEAR-CCOLI

DF, SF, GF, V, VG

- 3 pears
- 2 cups broccoli, cooked

Calories: 386
Carbohydrates: 97
Fat: 0
Protein: 9

GREEN APPLESAUCE

DF, SF, GF, V, VG

- 5 medium apples, cored
- 2 cups spinach
- 1/2 tsp cinnamon

Calories: 472
Carbohydrates: 125
Fat: 0
Protein: 2

BUTTERNUT SQUASH

DF, SF, GF, V, VG

- 1 large butternut squash, baked, skin and seeds removed
- 1 tsp dried sage (or 1 Tbsp fresh)

Calories: 328
Carbohydrates: 86
Fat: 0
Protein: 7

ONION PUREE

DF, SF, GF, V, VG

- 6 onions, sautéed

I know what you're thinking. "Onions?!"
    Onions are wonderful for gut health among other things. Freeze this recipe into very small cubes and mix into other vegetable based recipes or even entrees for a nice, nutrient boost.

Calories: 264
    Carbohydrates: 61
    Fat: 0
    Protein: 7

ROASTED VEGGIES

DF, SF, GF, V, VG

- 1 cup carrots, roasted
- 1 cup green beans, roasted
- 1 cup cauliflower, roasted
- 1 cup broccoli, roasted
- 1/4 cup olive oil

Calories: 174
Carbohydrates: 34
Fat: 0
Protein: 10

PEACH SALSA

DF, SF, GF, V, VG

- 6 peaches, peeled and seed removed
- 1/2 red onion
- 1/2 red bell pepper
- 2 Tbsp lime juice
- 1 Tbsp cilantro

Calories: 301
Carbohydrates: 73
Fat: 1
Protein: 6

SQUASHED BEETS

DF, SF, GF, V, VG

- 2 cans beets*
- 1 large butternut squash, baked, seeds and skin removed

*Always read ingredients to be sure you are only purchasing beets. Some canned beets contain high fructose corn syrup and other ingredients that are best avoided.

Calories: 408
Carbohydrates: 102
Fat: 0
Protein: 0

DESSERTS AND TREATS

STRAWBERRY SHORTCAKE

DF*, SF, GF**, V*, VG

- 2 pounds strawberries
- 10 slices whole grain bread
- 2 cups chickpeas
- 1 cup sugar
- 1 cup milk

*For dairy free and/or vegan, use dairy alternative.
**For gluten free, use gluten free bread.

Strawberry Shortcake	Calories	Carbohydrates	Fat	Protein
Strawberries	290	70	2	6
Bread	1000	200	10	30
Chickpeas	420	70	7	21
Sugar	720	192	0	0
Milk	160	13	8	8
Total	2590	545	27	65

VANILLA PUDDING

SF, GF, VG

- 3 cups coconut milk (carton)
- 1/2 cup sugar
- 3 Tbsp corn starch
- 1/4 cup cream

Calories: 890
Carbohydrates: 138
Fat: 39
Protein: 3

NUTTY BARS

DF, SF*, V, VG

- 12 oz bag semisweet chocolate chips
- 1 1/2 cups natural peanut butter
- 12 whole wheat saltines
- 2 cups soy milk

*For SF, replace with other dairy alternative

Calories: 4,282
   Carbohydrates: 353
   Fat: 249
   Protein: 110

FRUIT PIES

DF, SF, GF*, V, VG

- 1 pie crust, prepared according to package directions
- 2 cups blueberries
- 1/4 cup maple syrup

*For GF, use gluten free pie crust

Calories: 1,148
  Carbohydrates: 206
  Fat: 40
  Protein: 0

BUTTERY POPCORN

SF, GF, VG

- 1 cup whole milk
- 1/4 cup water
- 4 Tbsp butter
- 1/4 tsp salt
- 12 cups popcorn*

*Nutrition calculated based on air-popped popcorn

Calories: 939
Carbohydrates: 87
Fat: 59
Protein: 20

CHOCOLATE LEMON BROWNIES

DF, SF, GF, V, VG
Brownie Batter:

- 2 cups old fashioned oats
- 1 medium banana
- 1/2 Tbsp baking powder
- 1/2 Tbsp baking soda
- 4 cups red beans, prepared
- 2 Tbsp maple syrup
- 1/2 cup dates
- 1/2 cup water
- 1/3 cup cocoa powder
- 1/2 cup cashews
- 1/2 cup unsweetened coconut
- 1/4 cup chia seeds
- 1 cup dairy alternative
- Zest and juice of 2 lemons

Frosting:

150 | CHOCOLATE LEMON BROWNIES

- 2 cups dairy alternative
- 5 Tbsp tapioca flour
- 6 Tbsp lemon juice
- 1 cup cashews
- 2 tsp vanilla
- 1/4 cup maple syrup
- 6 dates

Run ingredients for batter in a food processor together. Press into cake pan lined with parchment paper. Bake at 350 degrees for 30 minutes.

Run frosting ingredients in blender for several minutes until thick. Top brownies. Cut into servings and blend into milk or dairy alternative (milk or dairy alternative for blending not included in nutritional information).

Calories: 3,899
    Carbohydrates: 546
    Fat: 147
    Protein: 105

BOOSTERS

BOOSTERS ARE INTENDED to increase the calories of a puree with only a small increase in volume. I recommend freezing these recipes into individual ice cubes to be thawed and added to individual servings of purees as needed to increase calories.

SUNFLOWER CREAM

DF, SF, GF, V, VG

- 3/4 cup water
- 1 cup sunflower seeds

Calories: 818
Carbohydrates: 28
Fat: 72
Protein: 29

CASHEW CREAM

DF, SF, GF, V, VG

- 1 1/2 cups cashews
- 1 cup water

Calories: 841
Carbohydrates: 42
Fat: 63
Protein: 29

WALNUT CREAM

DF, SF, GF, V, VG

- 2 cups walnuts
- 1 1/2 cups water

Calories: 1600
Carbohydrates: 32
Fat: 160
Protein: 40

PECAN CREAM

DF, SF, GF, V, VG

- 2 cups pecans
- 3/4 cup water

Calories: 1368
Carbohydrates: 27
Fat: 142
Protein: 18

BEVERAGES

BLUEBERRY SHAKE

DF, SF, GF, VG

- 1/2 medium banana
- 1/4 cup blueberries
- 1/4 cup baby spinach
- 1 Tbsp honey
- 10 cashews
- 1/4 cup cherry juice
- 1/2 cup vanilla Ripple milk

Calories: 328
Carbohydrates: 63
Fat: 9
Protein: 6

STRAWBERRY SHAKE

DF, SF, GF, VG

- 1/2 medium banana
- 1/4 cup strawberries
- 1/4 cup baby spinach
- 1 Tbsp honey
- 2 Tbsp sunflower seeds
- 1/4 cup cherry juice
- 1/2 cup vanilla ripple

Calories: 321
Carbohydrates: 55
Fat: 9
Protein: 7

PB & J SMOOTHIE

DF, SF, GF, VG

- 1/2 cup strawberries
- 1 banana
- 2 Tbsp cup peanut butter
- 1/2 cup almond milk
- 1/2 Tbsp honey

Calories: 399
Carbohydrates: 47
Fat: 17
Protein: 9

DAILY DOZEN SMOOTHIE

DF, SF, GF, V, VG

- 1 cup dairy alternative
- 1/4 cup berries
- 1 cup chopped fruit
- 1/4 cup kale
- 4 baby carrots
- 1/2 cup chopped cucumber
- 1/2 cup baby spinach
- 1/2 Tbsp ground flax seed
- 2 Tbsp nuts/seeds of choice
- 1 Tbsp peanut butter
- 1 Tbsp maple syrup

This smoothie was inspired by Dr. Michael Greger's Daily Dozen recommendations. Consisting of foods he recommends we strive to consume daily, this smoothie will meet your child's daily dozen in a large beverage that can be consumed throughout the day.

Calories: 415
  Carbohydrates: 41
  Fat: 21
  Protein: 9

PEANUT BUTTER BANANA SMOOTHIE

DF, SF, GF, VG

- 1 banana
- 1/2 cup almond milk
- 2 Tbsp peanut butter
- 1/2 tsp vanilla extract
- 1 Tbsp honey
- 1/4 cup baby spinach

Calories: 405
Carbohydrates: 50
Fat: 17
Protein: 9

KIDS KOFFEE

DF, SF, GF, VG

- 1/2 cup water, warmed
- 1/4 cup canned coconut milk
- 1 Tbsp molasses
- 1 Tbsp honey

Calories: 140
Carbohydrates: 31
Fat: 0
Protein: 1

STRAWBERRY PEACH SMOOTHIE

SF, GF, V, VG

- 1/2 cup strawberries
- 1 peach
- 1/2 cup coconut water
- 1/4 cup walnuts

Calories: 259
Carbohydrates: 21
Fat: 19
Protein: 5

RAZZLE RED SMOOTHIE

DF, SF, GF, V, VG

- 1/2 cup raspberries
- 1/2 cup blueberries
- 1/2 cup pineapple
- 1 cup canned coconut milk

Calories: 458
Carbohydrates: 30
Fat: 36
Protein: 0

CHAVOCADO SMOOTHIE

DF, SF, GF, V, VG

- 1/4 medium avocado
- 1/2 medium banana
- 1 Tbsp cocoa powder
- 2 Tbsp cup peanut butter
- 1/2 cup almond milk
- 1 Tbsp maple syrup
- 1/2 tsp vanilla extract

Calories: 443
Carbohydrates: 36
Fat: 25
Protein: 9

BLUE AVOCADO

DF, SF, GF, V, VG

- 1/4 avocado
- 1/3 cup blueberries
- 1/2 banana
- 1/4 cup oatmeal, cooked*
- 1/2 Tbsp ground flax seed
- 1 cup almond milk

*Measured Before cooking

Calories: 337
Carbohydrates: 47
Fat: 9
Protein: 2

PEACH CARROT SMOOTHIE

DF, SF, GF, VG

- 2 peaches, chopped
- 10 baby carrots
- 1/2 banana
- 1/2 cup coconut water
- 1/2 Tbsp honey
- 2 Tbsp sunflower seeds

Calories: 317
Carbohydrates: 58
Fat: 7
Protein: 6

CHOCOLATE PEANUT BUTTER SMOOTHIE

DF, SF, GF, VG

- 1/2 banana
- 1/2 cup baby spinach
- 1 cup almond milk
- 2 Tbsp peanut butter
- 1 Tbsp cocoa powder
- 1 Tbsp chia seeds
- 1 Tbsp honey
- 1/2 tsp vanilla
- 1/4 cup semisweet chocolate chips

Calories: 732
Carbohydrates: 82
Fat: 36
Protein: 14

PEACH QUINOA SMOOTHIE

DF, SF, GF, V, VG

- 1/4 cup quinoa, cooked*
- 2 peaches, chopped
- 1 cup almond milk
- 1/4 cup walnuts
- 1 Tbsp maple syrup

*Measure before cooking

Calories: 570
Carbohydrates: 65
Fat: 21
Protein: 12

PUMPKIN PIE SMOOTHIE

DF, SF, GF, VG

- 1/2 cup pumpkin puree
- 1/2 banana
- 1/2 cup almond milk
- 1 Tbsp honey
- 1/4 tsp vanilla
- 2 tsp pumpkin pie spice
- 10 pecans

Calories: 363
Carbohydrates: 43
Fat: 17
Protein: 4

MISC

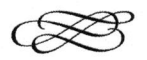

DAIRY FREE BUTTER

DF, SF, GF, V, VG

- 1 1/4 cup dairy alternative
- 2 cups cauliflower, cooked
- 1/8 tsp turmeric
- 1 tsp salt
- 1 tsp psyllium husks
- 2 Tbsp white miso
- 1/2 cup cashews

Calories: 504
Carbohydrates: 35
Fat: 21
Protein: 12

RANCH POWDER

SF, GF, VG

- 1/3 cup powdered buttermilk
- 2 Tbsp dried parsley
- 1 1/2 tsp dried dill weed
- 2 tsp garlic powder
- 2 tsp dried onion powder
- 3 tsp dried onion flakes
- 1 tsp black pepper
- 1 tsp salt

Calories: 106
Carbohydrates: 17
Fat: 0
Protein: 6

SALAD DRESSING

DF, SF, GF, V, VG

- 1/3 cup tahini
- 1/2 cup chopped green onion
- 2 Tbsp low sodium soy sauce
- 2 Tbsp rice vinegar
- juice from 1/2 lemon
- 1/4 tsp salt
- 3 roasted garlic cloves
- 1/4 cup olive oil
- 1/3 cup water

Calories: 998
Carbohydrates: 30
Fat: 98
Protein: 15

DAIRY FREE CHEEZE

DF, SF, GF, V, VG

- 1 cup potatoes, chopped and boiled
- 1 cup carrots, peeled and chopped and boiled
- 1/2 cup water
- 1/3 cup olive oil
- 2 tsp salt
- 1 Tbsp lemon juice
- 1/2 cup nutritional yeast
- 1 onion, sautéed
- 4 roasted garlic cloves

Add to dishes for flavor.

Calories: 1,000
 Carbohydrates: 63
 Fat: 76
 Protein: 22

DAIRY FREE TACO CHEEZE

DF, SF, GF, V, VG

- 1 cup cashews
- 1/2 cup water
- 1/4 cup tahini
- 1 Tbsp white miso
- 1 Tbsp dijon mustard
- 1 tsp chili powder
- 1 1/2 tsp cumin
- Juice from 2 lemons
- 1/4 tsp turmeric
- 2 tsp salt
- 1/2 tsp paprika
- 1 tsp garlic powder
- 1/4 cup nutritional yeast

- 1 cup water
- 1 Tbsp agar agar

202 | DAIRY FREE TACO CHEEZE

Blend top list of ingredients in blender. Place water in small saucepan and bring to a boil. Add agar agar and stir until dissolved. Add to blender and blend again. Pour into bowls and set in refrigerator. Cheese will harden as it cools.

Add to dishes for flavor

Calories: 986
    Carbohydrates: 49
    Fat: 73
    Protein: 41

DAIRY FREE SMOKEY CHEDDAR CHEEZE

DF, SF, GF, V, VG

- 1 cup cashews
- 1/3 cup water
- 1 Tbsp liquid smoke
- Juice from 2 lemons
- 1/4 cup tahini
- 1 small carrot, boiled
- 2 tsp salt
- 1/2 tsp smoked paprika
- 1 Tbsp dijon mustard
- 1/4 cup nutritional yeast
- 1 tsp garlic powder

- 1 cup water
- 1 Tbsp agar agar

Blend top list of ingredients in blender. Place water in small saucepan and bring to a boil. Add agar agar and stir until dissolved. Add to blender and blend again. Pour into bowls and set in refrigerator. Cheese will harden as it cools.

Add to dishes for flavor.

Calories: 956
- Carbohydrates: 45
- Fat: 73
- Protein: 41

DAIRY FREE MOZZARELLA CHEEZE

DF, SF, GF, V, VG

- 1 cup cashews
- 3/4 cup water
- 2 Tbsp nutritional yeast
- 1 Tbsp miso
- 1 Tbsp lemon juice
- 1 tsp tahini
- 1 tsp onion powder
- 1 tsp apple cider vinegar
- 1 tsp salt

- 1 cup water
- 1 Tbsp agar agar

Blend top list of ingredients in blender. Place water in small saucepan and bring to a boil. Add agar agar and stir until dissolved. Add to blender and blend again. Pour into bowls and set in refrigerator. Cheese will harden as it cools.

Add to dishes for flavor.

Calories: 620
- Carbohydrates: 34
- Fat: 42
- Protein: 20

ROASTED GARLIC

To roast garlic cloves, peel and discard the papery, outer layers of a garlic bulb, chop off the top portion (each garlic clove inside should be exposed), and top with a small amount of olive oil. Place on a baking sheet (cut side up), cover with foil, and bake at 400 degrees for 30-40 minutes. Allow to cool. Squeeze each individual section to pop out the bulbs.

    I like to bake several garlic bulbs at once and freeze them in a large container.

Made in the USA
Monee, IL
23 July 2020